The Gate Escape

A play about truancy

by Mark Wheeller

dbda

The Gate Escape
by Mark Wheeller

Commissioned and First Produced by The Haymarket Theatre, Basingstoke.

Author's acknowledgments:

Students from Cranbourne School, Basingstoke, particularly "Corey" and "Ali" for giving me their words and permission to re-tell their stories.

Development team from Haymarket (Basingstoke) and Oaklands (Southampton) Youth Theatres for their work in helping to generate some material for the play.

Anita Andrews; Alex Chalk; Katie Frecknall; Hollie Green; Arjun Malhotra; Elliot Roberts; Katie Smith, Danny Sturrock; Stephanie Tarry.

Brendon Burns for suggesting that I should be offered the commission in the first instance… and subsequent assistance in developing the play through discussion and rehearsals. His multi-media input has dragged Wheellerplays (kicking and screaming!) into the 21st Century!

Tim Wills – Haymarket Theatre

Julie Alden – Team Manager, Basingstoke Education Welfare Office.

Ann Morrison – Headteacher Cranbourne School.

Chris Vaudin – Head of Drama Cranbourne School.

Andy Kempe for suggestions following the pilot tour.

Evie, Dawn & Bharti from dbda who are always so willing to consider my plays for publication.

Meg Davis and all at MBA for their continued support and belief.

Roy Nevitt (Stantonbury Campus) for his inspiration in the use of Documentary theatre… "Dig Where you Stand".

My wife, Rachel, and children (Ollie, Charlie & Daisy) for love and support… and tolerance of long working hours.

Published by **dbda** 2004. First edition.

ISBN 1 902843 14 2

British Library Cataloguing in Publication Data
A catalogue record for this book is available from the British Library.

© Mark Wheeller 2003. Copyright is strictly reserved.
The moral right of the author has been asserted.

No part of this publication may be transmitted, stored in a retrieval system or reproduced in any form or by means electronic, mechanical, photocopying, typescript, recording or otherwise, without prior permission of the copyright owner.

Photocopying of scripts is illegal! Even if you hold a licence from the Copyright Licensing Agency you are only allowed to photocopy up to a total of 5% of the whole script. Please remember the writers who depend upon their share of your purchases… without them the plays which you perform could not have been written or published.

Enquiries regarding all rights associated with this play should be addressed to: Meg Davis, MBA Literary Agents Limited, 62 Grafton Way, London W1P 5LD. Tel: 0171 387 2076 Fax: 0171 387 2042.

Further copies of this publication can be purchased from:
dbda, Pin Point, 1-2 Rosslyn Crescent, Harrow HA1 2SB.
Tel: 0870 333 7771   Fax: 0870 333 7772   E-mail: info@dbda.co.uk

Introduction: the play in performance
By Brendon Burns, Director of the inaugural TIE production

'The Gate Escape' began its life as a result of a casual conversation between a community police officer and Tim Wills, the then Theatre Manager of the Haymarket Theatre, Basingstoke. If I remember the story correctly, Tim mentioned some recent success of the Theatre's education programme and the police officer expressed an interest in the development of a project which looked into the problems of truancy. I was the Associate Director of the Haymarket at the time and had just finished directing a TIE programme for Year 7 focusing on the difficulties of moving between Primary and Secondary School. We were just beginning to look at possible subjects for the following year when Tim relayed this conversation to me. It didn't take a huge amount of research to realise that truancy was an extremely pertinent, and indeed potent, subject for a Theatre in Education programme. We convened a steering group with representatives from schools, education welfare and the local community safety committee to develop the project for Year 8 and identify funding. During my time at the Haymarket I had written or devised most of our TIE work but as I was about to leave it was necessary to commission a writer. Given the successes of 'Too Much Punch for Judy', 'Hard to Swallow' and 'Legal Weapon' (amongst others) Mark Wheeller was an obvious choice. I was asked to return in a freelance capacity to direct the piece.

After interviews with a number of both persistent and 'reformed' truants, a series of workshops with Oaklands and Haymarket Youth Theatres and a lot of research, some interesting problems came to the fore. For a start, who should the piece be aimed at? Serious truants, by definition, may never see the play! Neither could it be a cautionary tale – don't truant or you might get run over by a bus, never pass your exams and then fall into a life of crime. Like all 'just say no' approaches that would be doomed to failure. There are far too many successful self-confessed truants for a simple 'don't do it' to have any effect at all. Certainly statistics suggest that a large number of young offenders regularly truant. But it would be an oversimplification to suggest that truancy leads to crime per se. Surely

Introduction

truanting and criminal behaviour are both symptoms of numerous other, perhaps more deep rooted, problems. Could we hope to tackle them all in one play! And what about the parent condoned truant? Technically, any unauthorised absence from school is defined as truancy. The causes of truancy are altogether far too complex and various for a simple solution.

As the play developed a dilemma began to emerge. What was more important, remaining true to the testimony of the 'real' truants – telling their story? Or ensuring that the piece would address issues that the audience could relate to, bearing in mind that the majority of the audience would not be serious truants themselves. Skillfully, Mark wove the nature of this dilemma into the structure of the piece itself. The story centres on two characters who truant – Corey claims to be "addicted", and Chalkie who views himself as a casual truant who only ever bunks to avoid trouble. The play explores their past on the day of their final truant together when they are greeted by a surreal 'Big Brother' like figure who sets them a task. The loser will be in for some dramatic Big Bother... who will lose... what will this bother be?

The play demanded a fast paced, multi-locational style which allowed for intense drama, open and frank participation, and humour. At my first meetings with the designer, Amy Mabire, we both agreed that the play itself didn't need a set. Indeed anything used to physically realise a location would slow the play enormously. We concentrated instead on creating the best possible space for participation. The audience were placed in an open thrust staging made up of four blocks of seating, each with three rows – the last row being raised. In this way we could ensure everyone could see, no one was more than two chairs away from stepping on to the stage and we had four ready-split groups for discussions and participation. By using Harris fencing to surround both the audience and the performing area we also created a separate space – somewhere that wasn't the school hall. At the same time it resembled a school fence with the resonance of being locked in – or, indeed, locked out as the case

The Gate Escape

may be. On stage, only four wooden cubes were used in a variety of combinations to create benches and seats. They had hinged lids which in addition to facilitating the storage of hand props also meant the blocks could become computers/toilets/lockers or have their lids loudly slammed for various effects.

Additionally, we used a back projection screen with a data projector linked to a laptop. This, very versatile set up, allowed us to use titles and icons to suggest location, to play short video clips (as part of the reality tv pastiche) and to use shadow play. It was also central to the participation strategies used.

It had been decided early in the process that the participation techniques used in The Gate Escape should aim to not only explore the issues and provoke discussion about truancy, but also to find out what the participants themselves thought the school (and other bodies) should do about the problem. Our opening pitch to the participants was "We are not really here to tell you anything – we want you to tell us". As discussed above we didn't want to deliver a message, we wanted dialogue.

We stopped the play at several key points to reflect, interrogate and expand understanding (both ours and theirs) of the events on stage. This took the form of small group discussions, hot seating, image theatre, forum theatre, list making and open debate. On the second tour (this time in co-production with Solent Peoples Theatre) we were fortunate enough to have the use of an Audience Response System(ARS). Each participant was equipped with an infrared handset which allowed them to vote anonymously on certain issues or questions throughout the performance. Their response was simultaneously calculated by the laptop and displayed as a bar graph or pie chart on the screen. By framing the participation dialectically within the dilemma of choosing which of the two protagonists were more justified in their truancy and by carefully selecting the moment and subject of each vote, we could ensure the participants both engaged in a point by point analysis of the plays themes and were

Introduction

able to respond to them. Used together with conventional methods of participation, the boisterous and the shy had their say, both the group and the individual were heard. The ARS stored all of the data from each individual in each performance and all this information, together with that gathered by conventional means, was passed back to the schools and to other relevant agencies.

To date, the play has toured twice to Hampshire schools and has met great success. This is in no small part due to the superb cast I was lucky enough to work with on both tours and I am extremely grateful to them. The play we performed was slightly different to the one that follows (to allow for participation) but the essence remains the same. This was best expressed by a participant responding to the question "Are all truants losers?" to which he replied "No… all truants are choosers". Are they? You decide!

Brendon Burns
Artistic Director, Solent Peoples Theatre

Oct 2003

Cast list in order of appearance

If performed by a cast of 2m, 2f this provides a guide as to which cast member should take on the role.

Chalkie White	A boy in Year 10	M1
Ali	A girl in year 10	F2
Beet	A boy in Year 10	M2
Corey Hudson	A (new) girl in Year 10	F1
Truants 1-3		M2, F1 & 2
Motorbike Boys 1-3		M2, F1 & 2
Steph	A girl in Year 9	F2
Steph's Mum		F1
Corey's Teachers 1-4		All
Voice	Off stage all the time	N/A
Isolate		F1
Chalkie's Dad		M2
Chip	Boy/Girl in Year 7	M1
Bunk	Boy/Girl in year 7	F1
Wag	Boy/Girl in Year 7	F2
Year 11 Student		F2
Billy	Corey's boyfriend	M1 or M2
Sue	Corey's Mum	F2
Mike	Corey's Dad	M2
Chalkie's Teachers 1-4		All
Mrs Picklewitch	Chalkie's English teacher	F2
Peter Performer	Star of School Plays at Chalkie's school	M2
Other children at the audition		N/A
Deathwish O'Connor	Year 10 girl (School Bully)	M2
Big Beanie	Deathwish's sidekick	F1
Little Beanie	Deathwish's sidekick	F2
Jayne	Corey's Aunt	F2
Terry	Superstar guitarist boy in Year 10	M2
Police 1 & 2		M2 & F2
TV Film Crew		All

A participatory version of THE GATE ESCAPE was first performed in a co-production by the Haymarket Theatre and Solent Peoples Theatre, in Spring and Autumn Terms 2003.

Cast:

Chalkie:	Owen Brazendale
Corey:	Lucy Holtom / Sarah Niven
Ali:	Sarah Hogarth
Beet:	Alexander Walker

All other parts played by the cast.

'Voice' & Technical operator:	Phillip Dundee
Director:	Brendon Burns
Designer:	Amy Mabire
Producer:	Haymarket Theatre

Section 1: Chalkie's Final Bunk (I)

MUSIC plays loudly. **Chalkie, Ali & Beet** *run on followed by* **Corey**, *who remains slightly behind the others as they arrive on stage and play with a range of discarded objects. These might include a lampshade, an old tyre, a ball, a torn and muddy office chair on wheels (makes a fantastic helicopter when turned upside down!), fold-up chair, a worn out suitcase (which could have anything in it!), a rolled up rug and a plastic milk crate.*

They use these objects in a range of imaginative ways setting up a high energy start to the play with mini scenarios generating an idea of the fun they are having. Finally they use this "rubbish" to set up their home/den (cotchment). They settle.

Chalkie:	I'd love to be in a Big Brother for teenagers… you know, our age!
Ali:	You'd be funny.
Chalkie:	I'd love it.
Beet:	Chalkie, who'd want to watch you for 9 weeks?
Ali:	It'd be a laugh.
Chalkie:	I bet you would watch it Beet…
Beet:	I'd vote you out mate!
Chalkie:	Thanks a lot.
Ali:	£70,000*… just think what you could do with that!
Beet:	They wouldn't have a big prize like that, it'd be more like…
All:	… a ten quid WH Smith's voucher!
Chalkie:	I'd do it for that… no probs… I'd do it for nothing!
Ali:	But if you did win seventy grand, it'd change your life.
Chalkie:	The prize doesn't matter to me!
Beet:	I'd hate it… everyone looking at you…
Chalkie:	That's what I'd like about it!
Beet:	… knowing everything about you?

* Update this figure accordingly.

Section 1

Chalkie:	Nothing to hide!
Ali:	What about you Corey?
Corey:	What?
Ali:	Would you want to go on Big Brother?
Corey:	Trapped in a house for eight weeks… no thanks!
Ali:	You're not really trapped.
Corey:	You are… it's like school.
Beet:	I'm glad they ain't got cameras in classrooms.
Ali:	That'd be scary!
Corey:	They can't… it's a human rights thing…
Chalkie:	I've got the video all sorted out.
Beet:	What video?
Chalkie:	The one you have to send off for Big Brother.
Beet:	You'd do a strip or something.
Chalkie:	No… they don't accept them if they're porny!
Beet:	They do… not like hardcore… I've seen some…
Chalkie:	Mine'd be a laugh. *(Chalkie hands a hand held camcorder to Ali who films him as he talks… the film is projected onto a screen 'live'.)*
Ali & Beet:	You're going to tell us all about it, aren't you Chalkie?
Chalkie:	You bet I am! I'd be on a Unicycle.
Beet:	*(Laughing.)* You can't ride one.
Chalkie:	I can learn.
Ali:	Beet… shut up… let him do it…
Beet:	It's minging!
Ali:	It's funny! Go on Chalkie…
Chalkie:	I'd be on my Unicycle and I'd say… I'd like to be in the Big Brother House 'cos I know

The Gate Escape

	I'm going to be a celebrity and this seems a good way of making it big time! I'm a singer in a band…
Beet:	Since when?
Chalkie:	Summer holidays.
Ali:	What are they called?
Chalkie:	The Ghostly Grasshoppers…
Ali & Beet:	Seventies or what?
Beet:	You sad git Chalkie!
Chalkie:	When I was five I had my palm read… and this old woman said that by the time I was 24 I'd be famous…
Ali:	Seriously Chalkie?
Chalkie:	No… but they won't know that…
Beet:	They don't like people going in just to get famous…
Chalkie:	Will I ain't gonna lie!
Beet:	What about the fortune teller?
Chalkie:	That's different!
Ali:	Ignore him Chalkie…
Chalkie:	Big Brother is my opportunity to make people laugh…
Beet:	That'll be a first!
Chalkie:	To give the girls something to get excited about…
Ali:	Go Chalkie!
Chalkie:	But more than anything… I'll guarantee to increase the viewing figures with my… I don't quite know what I'll say here… but… well what do you think?
Beet:	Chalkie… it sucks!
Chalkie:	*(Introducing Beet. The camera focuses on Beet.)* Then I'll have a bit where I'll introduce my mates… First Beet.
Beet:	I ain't a mate Chalkie… don't flatter yourself.

Section 1

Chalkie:	Beet is a moany old git… always complaining about something…
Beet:	That's better!
Chalkie:	Most people who meet Beet think his name is spelt… b.e.a.t… but no… b.e.e.t. Adam, that was his real name, was the only boy we knew, who liked beetroot… he had loads at his sixth birthday party *(Beet acts out what Chalkie describes… the others react.)* and then spewed a vibrant purple vomit all over his cake when he was blowing the candles out!
Beet:	Wicked, eh?
Chalkie:	From then on Adam was known as Beetroot… but it got shortened to Beet. *(He takes the camera from Ali and turns it on her.)* Ali… *(To the camera…)* I really fancied her… top totty of our school… of our neighbourhood… of the world!
Ali:	Shut up Chalkie!
Chalkie:	We'd gone out… but she chucked me…
Beet:	After three days wasn't it Chalkie?
Chalkie:	Four! She still liked me really… but… well… she got into drugs and stuff and I didn't really want to get involved. This is their cotchment… they come here when they're bunking off school… it's just a bush but they've put tyres, crates and stuff… like seats in it…
Beet:	We even double-glazed it!
Beet & Ali:	Double-glazed! *(Beet and Ali laugh.)*
Chalkie:	And this is Corey… *(Ali grabs the camera and zooms in on Corey.)* it's her first day here… she's a new girl…
Beet:	*(To Corey.)* How come you changed schools then?
Chalkie:	Not like ours is worth changing to…

The Gate Escape

Beet:	You got kicked out for causing trouble didn't ya?
Corey:	No!
Ali:	You did!
Ali, Beet & Chalkie:	What happened then?
Corey:	Nothing…
Ali:	Must have done.
Corey:	It didn't!
Beet:	No one comes to this school unless something bad's happened.
Chalkie:	And no one bunks on their first day…
Corey:	Well it hasn't!
Ali, Chalkie & Beet:	It was so obviously not the truth!
Chalkie:	*(Melodramatic American accent.)* …And… with my secret powers I could see straight through this tissue of lies. Corey had left her school because she had done something…
Ali, Chalkie & Beet:	Something dreadful!
Chalkie:	*(Enacts each with Ali or Beet.)*… poisoned her best friend… fallen madly, and passionately in love with…
Ali, Chalkie & Beet:	…the School Caretaker.
Chalkie:	Covered the Senior teachers in earwax and… gently set fire to them… *(sighs and suddenly reverts to normal voice delivering the line fairly quickly for comic effect.)* …or was it simply because she had an unusual name and weird hair. Anyway… that's it… I hope you choose me for Big Brother… you won't regret it if you do. Trust me! *(The camcorder is switched off at this point.)*
Ali:	Are you going to apply then?
Chalkie:	You've got to be eighteen.
Ali:	*(To Chalkie.)* I wish I was like you!
Beet:	What do you mean?

Section 1

Ali:	Clever.
Beet:	He ain't clever.
Ali:	Yeh but... good at school...
Chalkie:	Well I wish I was a bit more... I dunno... nothing seems to bother either of you... you don't care what people think.
Beet:	I'm glad I'm me. Wouldn't want to be either of you losers. I just wish I wasn't leaving!
Ali:	It's gonna be weird without you Beet. Well weird! *(Offering Corey a joint.)* Come on Corey...
Beet:	Leave her... it's a waste!
Corey:	*(Refusing politely.)* 's alright. I got fags. *(She takes out a cigarette [mimed] and lights it up.)*
Ali:	Don't you do these then? *(Corey shakes her head.)*
Beet & Ali:	We were always bunking.
Chalkie:	They used to say that as though it was some kind of achievement... like:
Beet & Ali:	We were always winning gold medals.
Beet:	Lessons for us were like very dull TV programmes...
Ali:	...which you can't switch off...
Beet:	To make it even more difficult they're all part of some long boring series...
Ali:	We'd missed so many episodes that we'd completely lost the plot...
Beet:	We just used to look forward to the commercial breaks as it were...
Ali:	By bunking... we could make the commercial breaks last as long as we wanted. *(To Corey.)* You don't say much.
Corey:	Not much to say, is there?
Ali:	I thought you'd be a laugh.
Beet:	Chalkie... catch this!

The Gate Escape

(He hurls an object at Chalkie and it develops into a game [or stylised movement sequence] denoting the passage of time. There could be a projection/ sign saying 'Ten Minutes later' and a short sequence of movement showing the three throwing something around, with Corey watching.)

Chalkie: My moment arrived to ask a highly charged and original question… the sort my mother would have been proud of. I moved with confidence to a place where everyone could see me… and stood up erect… like a… like an erect thing!
(Very cheesily!) Strange name… Corey… *(Clears throat … dramatically…)* What's its history?
(They all look at Chalkie perplexed.)

Ali, & Beet: What kind of a dumb question is that?

Corey: But he asks them so masterfully!

Chalkie: I remembered a lesson back in year 7: "Miss… What's circumcision?"

Beet: *(They all laugh.)* I cracked up when you asked that Chalkie?

Chalkie: It was in the Bible… you hardly expect…

Ali: Chalkie… it was a Maths lesson…

Ali & Beet: … circumference… *(They laugh.)*

Chalkie: Surprised you were there Ali… what was it?

Chalkie & Beet: First Maths lesson of the year?
(The passage of time sequence is repeated with the 'Ten Minutes later' caption. This time the sequence is noticeably slower.)

Chalkie: You know the bridge between Jeffrey's fruit shop and my house.

Ali: The bridge?

Chalkie: The wooden bridge…

Beet: The little wooden bridge?

Chalkie: I haven't exactly measured it. But you know it?

15

Section 1

Ali & Beet:	Yeh.
Chalkie:	Someone graffiti'd over it… must have been last night… dead neat… just writing…guess what it says.
Beet:	Something that rhymes with Chalkie is a banker?
Chalkie:	Funny Beet.
Ali:	Did they Chalkie?
Chalkie:	No.
Ali:	Oh.
Chalkie:	It's really weird.
Beet:	I can't wait for this.
Chalkie:	Well, if you don't want to know…
Ali:	I do!
Chalkie:	Forget it!
Beet:	Come on Chalkie… I was only joking!
Ali:	Chalkie what is it?
Chalkie:	I wish I'd kept quiet!
Beet:	Chalkie… I'm sorry… alright! So?
Beet & Ali:	What was the graffiti on the little wooden bridge?
Chalkie:	(As though writing.) "I hate this bridge."
Beet & Ali:	What?
Chalkie:	Why would someone write that? "I hate this bridge." Weird eh? Just made me… I dunno… feel sorry for the bridge!
Beet:	What I said was funnier!
Corey:	I wish I hadn't come.
Beet:	Why did you then?
Corey:	You said it'd be a laugh!
Ali:	's better than History!
Corey:	It ain't a laugh.

16

The Gate Escape

Chalkie:	What did you expect? Ronald MacDonald?
Ali & Beet:	Shut it Chalkie!
Corey:	I wish I'd stayed in school!
Beet:	Go back then!
Corey:	I might just… unless…
Ali, Beet & Chalkie:	Unless what?
Corey:	Dunno… but this is stupid!
Ali, Beet & Chalkie:	What?
Corey:	Babyish… this den…
Ali:	What do you want to do then, Corey?
Chalkie:	Now, I don't consider myself to 'proper' bunk… like regular… my problem was being easily led… you could say I suffered terminally from that… and I had a bad dose of it on this day… because before I knew where I was… we were all off, including me… out of the cotch and… on our way into town. Not what I intended to do at all… I was trying to avoid trouble… not create it!
Ali, Beet & Corey:	Chalkie… come on! Don't you ever stop narrating? *(They exit.)*
Chalkie:	As we made our way to town you'd be amazed at what we'd see… armies of truants…
Truants 1 & 2:	Attention! *(They pull up to attention.)*
Chalkie:	… well not an uniformed gun slinging army exactly… but a lot… some in groups like us…
Truants 1 & 2:	*(Chorally a la the Gumbies.)* We… like… terrorising people… throwing things … and… if we see anything good… we nick it… *(Truant 2 holds up a small tool.)*
Truant 2:	Look… a screwdriver!
Truant 1:	*(Truant 1 holds up a blueberry muffin.)* Look… a blueberry muffin.
Truant 2:	Gonna eat it?

17

Section 1

Truant 1:	Don't like blueberries!!!
Truant 2:	Der!
Chalkie:	*(Adopting the manner of a TV reporter.)* And what do you do if anyone annoys you?
Truants 1, 2 & 3:	*(Grinning broadly.)* We start a bit of aggro…
Chalkie:	And this is the moment where I think I can feel a bit of a slow motion action replay coming on… *(Loud music as they have a choreographed 'bundle'… in slow motion.)*
Chalkie:	Stop! The Bakery…
Others:	What?
Chalkie:	Didn't you notice?
Others:	No!
Chalkie:	Look!
Ali:	It isn't?
Others:	It is!
All:	You should be in school… tut tut tut!!!
Ali:	Not in there…
All:	… earning money!
Beet:	But we won't say nothing…
All:	If you chuck us a doughnut!
Chalkie:	Then, as we walk through the woods there are the boys with their motorbikes… *(Chorally Motorbike Boys 1-3 make the sound of a motorbike revving.)*
Motorbike boy 1:	First we nick the motorbikes… *(Chorally make the sound of revving.)*
Motorbike boy 2:	Then we ride 'em *(Chorally make the sound of revving.)*
Motorbike boy 3:	Off the road…
Motorbike boy 1:	On the road…

The Gate Escape

Motorbike boys:	In the woods! *(Chorally make the sound of revving.)*
Motorbike boy 3:	When they run out of petrol…
Motorbike boys:	*(Celebratory…)* We trash 'em! *(Chorally make the sound of revving… then spluttering to a halt, then an exaggerated mime of throwing the bikes up high in the air.)*
Motorbike boy 2:	*(Adopting a 'boffin' like voice.)* And then we go about fixing them. *(Becoming increasingly excited.)* Oh what fun!
Chalkie:	They may not do well at school…
Motorbike boys:	*(Beside themselves with excitement as 'boffins'.)* But we make fantastic mechanics!
Chalkie:	*(Adopting the excited manner of speech.)* Soon they have weaved their magic spell and without any petrol they ride off… into the distance… *(Back into normal delivery.)*
Motorbike boys:	No we don't… we go off into the woods! *(Chorally… the sound of revving and exit riding 'bikes' in different directions.)*
Chalkie:	I guess the most surprising… were the ones in town, not hiding… but… well… walking around… with their parents… *(Adopting the voice of the reporter again.)* Listen to Steph's story for example:
Steph:	I want to be a doctor so I know I've got to study hard for every test… today was no exception… I'd done my revision and I was getting ready for school… I had a Biology test and my Mum came in…
Steph's Mum:	You're not going to school today!
Steph:	I've got an exam.
Mum:	I'll write you a note!
Steph:	What? The note'll take the exam, will it?
Mum:	I thought you'd like to come shopping with me?

19

Section 1

Steph:	I don't want to.
Mum:	We never do anything together any more!
Steph:	I just picked up my bag and said… "I want to go to school!"
Mum:	I'll buy you an outfit for the party on Saturday.
Steph:	Already got one.
Mum:	Don't make me go on my own sweetheart. *(Melodramatic pause.)* I've been really lonely since daddy left.
Steph:	So I got changed and we went out shopping… *(With a forced smile.)* and I hated it… 'cos… 'cos I knew what'd happen. I'd go back to school armed with my note from Mum… and the teachers would say:
Teacher:	It's not a problem… You'll be able to do the test today… You can't help it if you're ill!
Steph:	And I just want to shout: "Look … I skipped school for the day… punish me!" *(Pause.)*
Chalkie:	As we approached the town centre… I spotted someone on their own… *(Isolate moves into this position.)* Hiding in the smelliest place imaginable…
All (except Isolate):	The Public toilets… Yuk!!! … surely even Maths is preferable to that…
Isolate:	No. Not if you're being bullied! **(Music:** *Images here of the Isolate being threatened/truants?)*
Chalkie:	So there we were… in the town centre… not by any stretch of the imagination the only ones who'd bunked off… which made what happened next all the more bizarre!
Voice:	*(Amplified with echo and high volume.)* Hello Chalkie.
Chalkie:	Hello?
Voice:	How are you today?

20

The Gate Escape

Chalkie:	I'm fine. Yeh good. Well, OK.
Voice:	How do you feel about what the group is doing at the moment?
Chalkie:	Well I…
Ali:	Chalkie?
Chalkie:	What?
Ali:	Who are you talking to?
Chalkie:	I don't know?
Ali:	Did you hear a voice?
Chalkie:	No.
Ali:	Chalkie… you did… 'cos I heard it too.
Corey & Beet:	And me!
Chalkie:	Seriously?
Others:	Yeh.
Ali:	Try and get it to speak again.
Chalkie:	What should I say?
Corey:	*(Confidently to the air.)* Hello there disembodied voice… how can we help you?
Voice:	Hello Corey.
Corey:	How the…?
Voice:	I am here to forewarn you of a dramatic end to your morning's truancy…
Chalkie:	Well, we'll go back then. *(They all turn to leave but are stopped in their tracks.)*
Voice:	Too late.
Chalkie:	What do you mean?
Voice:	There's no turning back… fate has decided.
Beet:	I've been caught loads of times before… it never bothers me… all that happens is:

Section 1

Teachers 1 & 2:	Where were you?
Teacher 1:	Where did you go?
Teacher 2:	What on earth were you doing?
Teachers 1 & 2:	You could have been killed!
Teacher 1:	People get into all sorts of trouble when they truant.
Teacher 2:	All sorts of trouble!
Teacher 1:	And, if there's a fire in the building, we don't know you're out of school…
Teacher 2:	Someone may go risking their lives searching for you…
Beet:	Was there?
Teachers 1 & 2:	That's not the point!
Teacher 1:	Now… just to show you how angry I am, I'm going to ask you to…
All:	*(Singing melodramatically.)* Dun Dun Dahr!!!
Teachers 1 & 2:	Give me your planner!!!
Teacher 2:	And if you think you're going out at Break and lunch time…
Teachers 1 & 2:	…you've got another think coming! *(Add an appropriately evil laugh! The cast group round to hear the reaction from the Voice.)*
Beet:	And that's all that happens… just a little bit of bother.
Voice:	Oh no! Today will be… "Big Bother"!
All:	Big Bother?
Voice:	Big Bother. *(Possibly this phrase is flashed up on the screen.)*
Beet:	Well it won't bother me… I'm leaving!
Corey:	We're all going to get really done?
Voice:	Not all of you.
All:	What?
Voice:	One of you shall face this "Big Bother" alone.

The Gate Escape

All:	One of us?
Voice:	Yes.
Chalkie:	I bet it's me.
Corey:	No it'll be me.
Ali:	I could do with a break… it's always me… even when it isn't!
Beet:	I don't mind 'cos I'm leaving anyway…
Chalkie:	Come on then…
Voice:	Fate has decided to select from two of you. All will be revealed when you complete your task.
All 4:	Task? What task?
Corey:	Look… there's a piece of paper there. *(They crowd round the laminate. Reading.)* Each of the group must nominate who shall face the Big Bother. The two group members with most nominations will have approximately one hour to convince Fate that they were justified in missing school today. The group member with the most successful justification will, along with the two not nominated, be released from any bother at all today. The least successful will face "Big Bother"… alone.
All:	Bloody hell!
Voice:	All members of the group should make their nominations. *(The following sequence should be pre-filmed and shown on a screen. The characters all run off stage as though to a 'diary' area/room.)*
Ali:	My first nomination is Corey… 'cos she's new… that one's easy… but the other… I don't know.
Chalkie:	Beet… 'cos he's really annoyed me today… and he's leaving.
Beet:	This is wicked! Can I vote for myself… 'cos I ain't got anything to lose?
Corey:	This is hard for me 'cos I hardly know them…

Section 1

	do I have to do it?
Beet:	Chalkie and Corey… Chalkie 'cos he's a… well you know… he's Chalkie… and Corey… 'cos she's wet.
Ali:	I don't know… I hate doing this!
Corey:	Alright then… Chalkie… just to stop him thinking I fancy him.
Chalkie:	It's not fair… I don't want to do it! What are you gonna do about it if I don't cast my nomination! Come on then… what are you gonna to do?
Ali:	Chalkie… not because of anything he's done… it's just that I don't want anything to happen to Beet… he's like my best mate… and this is his last day.
Corey:	Beet… 'cos he's been horrible to Chalkie… and Chalkie's cute!
Chalkie:	This won't get out… will it? Corey. 'Cos she's new… and… well I know Ali better and… I think she's trying to give me the cold shoulder.
Beet:	Chalkie… I really hope it's Chalkie… he'll be well gutted! *(Doing a one fingered salute to the camera)* … up yours Chalkie! *(The characters return to the stage.)*
Voice:	The nominations are complete. The decision has been made.
Chalkie:	Come on who is it? *(Silence.)*
Ali:	Come on!
Voice:	The two characters nominated to play for the right to avoid the Big Bother are… in alphabetical order: *(Silence.)*
Chalkie:	Get on with it.
Beet:	Don't know why you're all getting so stressed… it can't be that bad!
Ali:	So come on then!
Chalkie:	Yeh… who's it going to be?

The Gate Escape

Voice:	Chalkie and… *(Silence.)*
Beet:	Wicked!
Chalkie:	Oh no…
All:	Shut up Chalkie! *(Silence.)*
Ali:	It's gonna be me… it's gonna be me!
Corey:	Please don't let it be me!
Voice:	Corey.
Corey:	*(Sarcastically.)* Oh great!
Chalkie:	It's unfair…
Voice:	All of you chose to be here… fate can only choose from those who present themselves.
Chalkie:	I didn't.
All:	You did Chalkie…
Chalkie:	*(To Ali and Beet.)* You talked me into it!
Beet:	But you chose to come with us!
Ali:	Of your own free will.
Chalkie:	*(To Voice.)* Beet and Ali… they're always bunking… anyway… what is this ending?
Voice:	All will be revealed… when you complete the task.
Chalkie:	Come on then… lets get this over and done with.
Voice:	You first Chalkie!
Chalkie:	OK… and I hope the Voice notices this… I'm going first… please take that into consideration when making your decision! Right!

Section 2: Chalkie's First Bunk

All:	*(Adopting new positions/characters.)* Chalkie's first bunk!
Chalkie:	I had problems with swimming dating back to when I was four… my dad decided to teach me.
Chalkie's Dad (M2):	I just grabbed him… and…
All:	Threw him in the deep end!
Ali:	Thus a rubber ring became our hero's embarrassing companion in the water…
Chalkie:	So when I heard we had swimming one day in Year 6… I… well I had no choice.
Corey:	Bunking…
Beet:	Skiving…
Ali:	Chipping off…
Corey:	Wagging it…
Chalkie:	Or… to give it its proper handle…
All:	Truanting.
Corey:	Luckily some mates he knew from another school… *(Beet, Ali and Corey undergo a transformation becoming the friends – Chip, Wag and Bunk – possibly introducing themselves with their name and an individualistic motif.)* had the day off.
Chip:	What shall we do?
Bunk:	I know…
Others:	Yes?
Bunk:	You won't want to…
Others:	Try us…
Bunk:	Strip off and run round Simsbury's!
Chalkie:	You're right… we wouldn't want to…
Bunk:	Nick a car and drive to the beach?
Chalkie:	Too cold for the beach!
Chip:	"Knock door Ginger"?

The Gate Escape

Wag:	With our legs tied together?
Chalkie:	What?
Bunk:	Let's do the History Exam… I'm sure I have the paper somewhere… *(Starts rummaging around.)*
All:	*(As though they have suddenly been made members of the Famous Five!)* Gosh! What a spiffing idea!
Chalkie:	I'd rather set fire to Gary…
All:	Did that last week!
Chalkie:	I kept on thinking… "I'm going to get grounded for this if my parents find out!"… but it was worth it… my secret rubber ring relationship was safe…
All 4:	…Until…
Wag:	I know… let's go to the Sports Centre…
All (except Chalkie):	Yeh!
Bunk:	Swimming!
All (except Chalkie):	Fantastic idea. *(They slap their thighs a la panto!)* Last one in the water's a plonker! *(They run off and freeze [with a loud cheer] as though they are jumping in the water.)* Chalkie… aren't you coming?
Chalkie:	And that was that…
Corey:	No incurable medical condition…
Beet:	No psychological trauma…
Ali:	No broken home…
Chalkie:	In fact I came from a happy and contented home…
Ali:	He was well liked at school…
Chalkie:	More… more!
Ali:	Popular!
Chalkie:	Particularly with the girls?
Ali:	He was cool!

27

Section 2

Beet:	Nothing got him down.
Corey:	So, basically you're saying you had no excuse whatsoever for bunking!
Chalkie:	I was dependent on bunking... it was one super-sure way of avoiding problems.
Ali:	Enter "Problem". *(Physically blocks Chalkie.)*
Beet:	So... what does Chalkie do?
Corey:	*(Chalkie hammers at Ali.)* Try to batter it down?
All:	No!
Corey:	*(Chalkie converses 'at' Ali.)* Tries to talk it into submission.
All:	No!
Corey:	*(Chalkie makes Ali look in one direction and runs off in another.)* Plays a trick on it and runs off?
All:	No! No! and No again!
Corey:	So Chalkie... what do you do?
Chalkie:	I simply approach the problem... *(Approaches Ali.)* and if I can't see a resolution I side step it and calmly walk away. *(The others clap and cheer.)* So you see... I was lucky... nothing to do with my background or whatever... it was always down to a situation I found myself in ... and I'd only choose to bunk... if I needed to avoid some embarrassment... or trouble...
Corey:	Whereas me...

Section 3: Corey's Story

Corey:	Bunking was my drug. The risk of getting caught provided the buzz… if you walk round the corner and see the police… your heart goes and it's like a mad rush… but when you get away with it it's just… you're even more determined to do it again.
Chalkie:	"So Corey," says Chalkie putting on his best reporter voice: *(Over the top.)* "How did it all begin?"
Corey:	In year 6… my friend was doing it… but I was so scared of what my mum and dad would say… that I didn't do it again. I proper started bunking… whole days off… at Secondary school.
Ali:	It's harder at Junior School cos you only have one teacher… so you're noticed more easily.
Corey:	But when you get to Secondary School… it's… well it's so easy…
Chalkie:	Nobody knows you…
Corey:	It's so tempting… just to…
Chalkie:	All it needs is for…
Corey:	Something to happen…
Chalkie:	Could be anything…
Teacher:	Have you done your homework Corey Hudson?
Corey:	The budgerigar escaped last night Sir and then, while we were out looking for it, the neighbour's dog messed on my homework sir… I didn't think you'd want it all sticky and stinking of dog-pooh.
Teacher:	Don't try and pull the wool over my eyes.
Corey:	Do what?
Teacher:	You haven't done it, have you?
Corey:	No Sir.
Teacher:	If it happens again you'll have a detention…
Corey:	OK sir… thank-you sir.
Teacher:	Now be on your way… Corey *(Sensing danger.)*… be careful…

Section 3

Chalkie:	But he was too late....
Year 11:	A Year 11 student escaping from a supply teacher's nightmare... *(Enter like an out of control aeroplane...)* piles down the corridor... at what seems like a hundred miles an hour!
Corey:	Corey Hudson turns...
Chalkie:	But it's too late...
All:	Aaaargh!!!
Year 11:	The crash of Year 11 muscle into...
Corey:	Fragile Year 7 bones...
Teacher:	Echoes along the corridor...
All:	Corey's first flying lesson...
Corey:	She soars through the air...
Year 11:	And falls to the cheap marble effect floor with a mildly 'entertaining'...
All:	Crash!
Chalkie:	Heads poke out of doors to see what's going on as the Year 11 turns to speak to our hero.
Year 11:	That'll teach you to watch where you're going!
Chalkie:	And Corey Hudson is left alone to moisten the cheap marble effect floor with the wetness of her tears. Then, like a monster emerging from the dust she rises... and the silence is shattered by a desperate shrieking...
Corey:	I hate this bloody place... I hate it... nobody cares!
Chalkie:	Corey wanted to be anywhere but here...
Corey:	Anywhere...
Chalkie:	Home...
Beet:	Town...
Ali:	An orchard...
Chalkie:	Inside a sea-shell...

The Gate Escape

Beet:	Stuck to the slippery floor of an unwashed pig-sty…
Chalkie:	At her Gran's eating some rock-hard fruitcake.
Corey:	*(Warning.)* Chalkie!
Ali:	Corey wanted to be anywhere…
All:	… well almost anywhere…
Ali:	… but here!
Chalkie:	She thought things could never get any worse…
Corey:	*(Beet swiftly adopts the role of Corey's [very elderly] Granny. Corey looks up.)* Gran? What are you doing here?
Beet:	I've bought you some of that lovely fruitcake you like when you come round to mine!
Corey:	Beet!!!
Beet:	With cake and fruit in it…
Corey:	Beet!!! Take that ridiculous costume off and…
Beet:	Only having a laugh.
Corey:	Corey thought things could never get any worse …
All:	… but they did.
Chalkie:	At the start of Year 8 an announcement was made.
Corey:	I couldn't believe it… we were all being put in different classes… "grouped according to our ability"… I'd done well in my SATS back in Year 6 so I wasn't that worried… then…
Teacher:	Corey Hudson… you will be in the Muppet class, can you go over there.
Corey:	But Sir… I got good SATS results…
Teacher:	No Corey… these sets are based on your work in Year 7… not Year 6… you are in the Muppet class.
Corey:	But Sir… I want to be with Sue… I've been with her since reception!
Teacher:	Suzanne Swottalot, your best friend for the last

31

Section 3

	seven years, is to be in the Boffins class… well done Suzanne… but don't worry Corey… you'll probably still see her every now and then… PE… Drama… if she wants to be seen with a Muppet that is!
Corey:	I just thought… if they've decided I'm a Muppet… well what's the point? *(Corey remains in a still image pondering her future… and perhaps her past!)*
Chalkie:	So… Corey was ripe… ripe for bunking… everything in place… she just needed a… a catalyst… something… or someone… to trigger it into action…
Corey:	At Easter of Year 8, I started going out with this guy who was 15. *(Enter Billy. On skates, a big, over the top entrance with Music.)* Billy… went to a different school… well I don't think he 'went' much at all. I met him at the Park. We just got talking and it was… well… cool…
Billy:	Like my new skates?
Corey:	Your parents must be loaded. Mine'd never buy me anything like that.
Billy:	Interest free credit…
Corey:	What?
Billy:	Five-finger discount?
Corey:	I don't…
Billy:	Robbed them up.
Corey:	*(Loudly.)* Robbed them?
Billy:	Don't tell everyone!
Corey:	How often do you do it?
Billy:	What?
Corey:	Rob stuff.
Billy:	Any time…

The Gate Escape

Corey:	What about school?
Billy:	Chip off with me… up the shops…
Corey:	My Aunt works in town…
Billy:	Somewhere else… anyway it's better to be away…
Corey:	Bunk off school?
Billy:	It's a laugh… *(Melodramatically.)* How about tomorrow?
Corey:	*(Laughs.)* It was that easy. I'd nicked sweets before… but this was something else… he said it's just a…
Billy:	"Great big proper genuine rush!"
Corey:	I thought… a "great big proper genuine rush"… I'd love to do that! We met at 8 in the morning… I wore my black trousers and this nice top underneath my school uniform. I took a bag with my pens in it, and changed… put my clothes in the bag… Mum and Dad didn't suspect anything. *(Loud Music kicks in… Billy & Corey meet up… and through choreographed movement involving the other two actors show their day out "Robbing up". In the original production this was done using back projections to show the location/shops.)*
Corey:	What a day… thanks Billy.
Billy:	Told you it'd be a laugh.
Corey:	When can we go again?
Billy:	Monday?
Corey:	Cool.
Billy:	Bye… *(They kiss.)*
Corey:	My hero! I went home as if nothing had happened. Mum said:
Sue:	How was your day love?
Corey:	Brilliant!

Section 3

Sue:	Good… nice to hear you so positive for a change.
Corey:	Well… it was alright…
Sue:	Has something happened?
Corey:	No, it was fine honestly…
Sue:	You haven't forgotten your jumper, have you Corey?
Corey:	I didn't wear it…
Sue:	You'll catch a cold…
Corey:	Better than an STD?
Sue:	Pardon?
Corey:	Sexually transmitted disease… we've been doing about them in Health Ed.
Sue:	Yes… I see… it would be I suppose!
Corey:	Billy was nicking all the time… make-up, cd's, clothes… it got to the point where people'd give us a list of what to get for them… we'd get about £200 worth of stuff a day… and sell it on for about £30… who says money doesn't grow on trees? I could buy loads of fags… and not be paying for them. One week, in October… I was in year 9… we bunked off three days in a row. That's when my mum got involved…
Sue:	Corey?
Corey:	What have I done now?
Sue:	Have you been to school today?
Corey:	Course!
Sue:	So why did Mr Biscuit phone up and say you weren't there?
Corey:	Mr Biscuit is a plonker. You know he is. He sent me to the Medical room with Jenny… she'd had a nosebleed. He probably forgot…
Sue:	Well he could have phoned to let me know…
Corey:	He said he would…

The Gate Escape

Sue:	Well he didn't… I've a good mind to go up to that school and…
Corey:	Don't worry Mum… he's a pratt… everyone knows he is! Fortunately she never asked what was in my bag…
Sue:	So… what is in your bag then?
Corey:	Mum!!!
Sue:	Only joking…
Corey:	It was jam packed full of stolen stuff!
Sue:	Well if you do ever bunk… you'll be grounded.
Corey:	Everyone says my writing's like my mum's… so I forged notes… another little crime to add to my list!
Sue:	Suspecting what was going on, I went into school and gave them a different signature…
Corey:	The next day I went to hand my note in… the one I'd written… saying I'd had a doctors appointment…
Teacher 4:	That's not your Mum's signature.
Corey:	Well my mum writ (sic) it so it must be!
Teacher:	Your mum brought us a copy of her… her new signature… look…
Corey:	I got an hour's detention… but it did nothing to stop me from bunking.
Sue:	Then the arguments started…
Corey:	(As though arguing, stating the lines as though they are lines from the argument in the style that is described and building to a climax.) Ongoing…
Sue:	Taking up from the last time…
Corey:	… bringing stuff up from the past…
Sue:	… clutching at straws…
Corey:	… lying…
Sue:	… suspecting…

35

Section 3

Corey:	… but not proving…
Sue:	… not being able to prove anything…
Corey:	… provoking…
Sue:	… feeling frustrated…
Corey:	… defensive…
Sue:	… attacking…
Corey:	… shouting…
Sue:	… louder…
Corey:	… hurtful…
Sue:	… passionate…
Corey:	… swearing…
Sue:	… what has happened to you?
Corey:	… bad swearing… can't believe I'm saying this to my Mum… really bad swearing…
Sue:	We didn't bring you up like this Corey!
Corey:	… tearful…
Sue:	… out of control…
Corey:	… raising hands…
Sue:	… fists…
Both:	Fighting!
Corey:	Then dad got involved.
Mike:	*(To Sue.)* Why?
Sue:	*(Referring to Corey)* It's her.
Mike:	Why?
Corey:	*(Referring to Sue.)* It's her.
Corey & Sue:	Fighting!
Mike:	Why?
Corey & Sue:	*(To each other.)* It's her!
Mike:	*(Shouted.)* If you don't stop… I'm out of here!

The Gate Escape

	(Silence.)
Sue:	Corey… we can't go on like this…
Corey:	Well stop going on at me then!
Sue & Mike:	Can't you see… you're wasting your life?
Corey:	*(Turning in slow motion to the audience to say this line passionately.)* I'd hate it if I had to live life like you want me to.
Sue & Mike:	We can't go on like this.
Teacher 1:	Phone call from school…
Mike:	Answer.
Teacher 1:	Very polite introduction.
Mike:	Polite response.
Teacher 1:	Accusation.
Mike:	Corey?
Teacher 1:	Drugs.
Mike:	Drugs?
Corey:	I didn't take nothing.
Dad:	Not what they said.
Corey:	No proof… they're lying…
Mike:	You admit you were there.
Corey:	Yeh.
Mike:	Why?
Corey:	I wasn't feeling very well.
Mike:	You should have been in the sick room.
Corey:	It was too boring.
Sue:	And taking drugs was going to make everything alright was it?
Corey:	I don't do that stuff. The police found us… found a bong… they took it away… noted down our names…

Section 3

Mike:	I don't know what we've done to deserve all this?
Corey:	Chuck me out then… I know that's what you want to do… go on… chuck me out!
Sue:	*(Quietly.)* You know that's not what we want.
Corey:	But they chucked me out all the same.
	(Silence.)

Section 4: Chalkie's Life in Secondary School

Chalkie:	When I went on to Secondary School some of the teachers felt that they already knew me…
Teacher 1:	Oh… Marvin White's brother… **you'd** better come and sit at the front.
Chalkie:	Marvin was bright… so my Mum said… but
Teacher 2:	I've heard that name before… you're not related to…
Chalkie:	Marvin?
Teacher 3:	I'm surprised you own up to that… wasted his time here!
Chalkie:	"Can't choose your relations Sir." I said with an edge designed to annoy.
Teachers:	"Pity we can't choose our classes boy."
Teacher 1:	Said with teacher-trained sarcasm!
Chalkie:	And then… worst of all there was always the teacher who would initially try to… well… suck up…
Mrs Picklewitch:	*(As though a slimy monster.)* I used to have a good relationship with Marvin. I'm sure we'll get on.
Chalkie:	Roughly translates as:
Mrs Picklewitch:	*(In this 'translation' she changes character completely as her inner turmoil comes to the fore.)* I hated your brother… and because he was such a problem for me I'll take every opportunity to reek my revenge on you… and nothing you can do will stop me! Nothing!!! Ha ha ha ha ha!!! *(Evil laughter outstays its welcome!)*
Chalkie:	Marvin hated Mrs. Picklewitch… "Fortunately I'm not like my brother Miss *(sic)* Picklewitch."
Mrs Picklewitch:	Insolence! Wait outside the door. I'll deal with you later!
Chalkie:	I didn't say anything!
Mrs Picklewitch:	Don't argue! If this is what you are like on your first day I dread to think…
Chalkie:	What?

Section 4

Miss Picklewitch:	I'm not telling you again! Get out… NOW!!!
Chalkie:	This was made worse for me because Miss Picklewitch was organising the School Play, which would, I hoped, launch my showbiz career! I went to the audition full of confidence… to be greeted by:
Mrs Picklewitch:	Chalkie White? You must be in the wrong room!
Chalkie:	The auditions Miss?
Mrs Picklewitch:	Yes.
Chalkie:	The auditions for **Stanley Smang Slipped on a Banana Then Got Up Again!**
Mrs Picklewitch:	<u>You</u> will be auditioning for <u>my</u> play?
Chalkie:	Yes Miss.
Mrs Picklewitch:	If you must… there… take a seat at the front… by Peter Performer.
Chalkie:	Peter Performer always got the main parts in school productions but today he was having huge problems due to a dodgy curry he'd consumed the night before. It had been, to put it politely, a very 'windy' day for Peter!
Mrs Picklewitch:	We're going to do a read through… hands up if you would like to read the part of Shiney Smang? *(Chalkie and Peter put their hands up.)* Robert Readalot you do that one then. *(Hands down in disappointment.)* Smingy Smang? *(Hands up again with renewed hope.)* Primrose Perfect I think you'd do that nicely. *(Hands down in disappointment.)* Stanley Smang? *(Chalkie and Peter put their hands up.)* Now this is the main part… *(Chalkie strains to make his hand stretch further.)* Peter Performer… I think you should read this. *(Chalkie puts his hand down in disappointment.)*
Chalkie:	Each time I put my hand up… *(Chalkie punches his hand into the air.)*
Mrs Picklewitch:	Tiddley Smang? Adrian Actalot… I know you'll enjoy reading that role… it's a really funny part! He's there when Stanley slips over… it's… well

The Gate Escape

	you'll see... it's amazing!
Chalkie:	*(Chalkie slowly puts his hand down.)* I was ignored.
Mrs. Picklewitch:	Now, those of you who haven't been given a role...
Chalkie:	There was only me in this category...
Mrs Picklewitch:	Will have to follow it carefully in the book and then if you're good... we'll give you a chance to read later on.
Chalkie:	I'd be ignored completely, but I sat there in silence sharing Peter Performer's book envying his every line and occasionally having to inhale his silent but deadly ones. Then the unforgivable happened... during the speech which led to the tragic climax of the play... Stanley Smang slipping over...
Peter:	*(Reading.)* "Tiddley Smang... come here... now listen... when you finish that banana put the skin over there... in the bin...." *(Peter then makes a very loud 'farting' sound. He continues to read as though nothing has happened.)* "... or there could be a most terrible accident."
Mrs Picklewitch:	Chalkie White stand up.
Chalkie:	*(Standing.)* Yes Miss.
Mrs Picklewitch:	If you think you can come to these auditions to distract Peter Performer by making such a disgusting noise while he's reading his most important speech in <u>my</u> play... you've got another think coming.
Chalkie:	But it wasn't me Miss.
Mrs Picklewitch:	Well it came from your part of the room.
Chalkie:	I know Miss but it wasn't me!
Mrs Picklewitch:	Well would you like to tell me who it was then?
Chalkie:	No Miss. That'd be grassing.
Mrs Picklewitch:	How nice it would be if you could own up and at least be honest. None of us are impressed, are we?

Section 4

Chalkie: But Miss.

Mrs Picklewitch: Get out!!!

Chalkie: Most of the teachers took me for what I was… but Picklewitch, just used to look at me and see my brother… my brother on a bad day! The next day I bunked her lesson and then stayed off for the whole day in case she saw me… I got away with it.

Corey: That always happens…

Chalkie: But they found out in the end…

Corey: How?

Chalkie: I bunked off my next two English lessons… and on the second time she saw me during lunch.

Corey: What happened?

Chalkie: She reported it and I had to go and see the Head of Year… it was alright actually… she was nice… let me explain… then… made me promise not to do it again.

Corey: Did she tell your parents?

Chalkie: No… she said she wouldn't do that unless I bunked off again… and I didn't… if they found out they'd've gone mental! I reckon she knew what Picklewitch was like… *(Smiling.)* oh, there was one other time I bunked off her lesson…

Corey: *(Smiling.)* When?

Chalkie: On the day she left… she was having a baby. I went in really early that morning and wrote… "Picklewitch pregnant? Boy/girl… human/rhinoceros? Place your bets!"… on the board in her room… I didn't stay around… apparently she went ape…

Corey: Did you get found out?

Chalkie: I signed it so she knew alright… but nothing happened!

Corey: Someone like that can destroy all your dreams.

The Gate Escape

Chalkie: No school production was gonna to get me on EastEnders, was it? In any case it got cancelled when she found out she was pregnant... but talent will out! At the end of year 9, I signed on with an agent...

Corey: Wow!

Chalkie: Yeh... I had photos done...

Corey: To make you look attractive you mean?

Chalkie: Even more attractive... yeh.

Corey: Have you got any work?

Chalkie: They say it takes about a year... I've been with them six months now.

Corey: Aren't some of these agents conmen?

Chalkie: This one isn't... the signing on fee was only three hundred quid!

(The characters move into their new positions. A text message sound bleeps. A text message is revealed on screen or by Chalkie reading the message.) **Danzo wants 2 fight u**

Who sent that?

Ali: Just trying to freak you. Do you remember it?

Chalkie: I'll never forget that... another instance of bunking to avoid trouble. I remember you and Beet... *(Sarcastically.)* making me feel so much better!!!

Ali: You wanna watch your back Chalkie...

Beet: Danzo wants to fight you...

Chalkie: Danzo was two years younger than me... but he was... hard... mean... nothing scared Danzo.

Ali & Beet: He's very small.

Chalkie: But in a fight he really goes for it.

Ali & Beet: When we saw him in a fight...

Ali: His victim went down...

43

Section 4

Beet: And Danzo went in even harder…

Ali: He had to be forcibly torn away.

Beet: But he is small, Chalkie.

Ali: And the lad he was fighting was small too.

Beet: You're bigger than him Chalkie.

Ali: You could have him.

Beet: Get him on his own.

Ali: You'd be a hero if you did Chalk!

All: Just imagine if Chalkie did sort him out.

Beet: The next day… Chalkie walking into school would be like…

Ali: Everyone turning…

Beet: Cheering…

Ali: Bowing.

Beet: Making a path for Chalkie…

Ali: Just like Moses parting the Red Sea.

Beet: Who?

Ali: Moses… in the Bible… he made a path through the middle of the sea to help get his people to the Promised Land.

Chalkie: *(Scared.)* But he wears rings…

Beet: Who Moses?

Chalkie: No, Danzo you plonker!

Ali: Yeh… rings that cut…

Beet: Lacerate skin.

Ali: He isn't scared of the consequences.

Chalkie: Nothing seems to scare Danzo.

Beet: But you mustn't let people know he frightens you.

Ali: Not someone in Year 7.

The Gate Escape

Beet:	Two years younger than you!
Ali:	You've got to face him Chalkie…
Ali & Beet:	You've got to face him!
Corey:	How come he was so angry?
Beet:	*(To Chalkie.)* You know that ball you found…
Ali:	The ball you wrote **your** name on Chalkie…
Beet:	Even though you knew it wasn't yours…
Chalkie:	Yeh…
Ali & Beet:	It was Danzo's.
Chalkie:	I dunno where it is!
Ali & Beet:	Danzo wants his ball back!
Corey:	How stupid!
Chalkie:	*(To Ali & Beet.)* I lost it!
Beet:	You'd better find it.
Ali:	You wanna watch your back Chalkie…
Chalkie:	Then the message came through again: **Danzo wants 2 fight u…2moro…**
Corey:	All over a ball?
Chalkie:	Maybe… but the thought of a Year 7 showing me up…
Ali & Beet:	*(Grabbing at Chalkie and lifting him up by the scruff of his neck.)* Beating you up…
Chalkie:	Alright… alright…
Ali & Beet:	*(Threatening.)* Say it then…
Chalkie:	Alright… beating me up. *(They throw him down.)* Well it didn't really appeal… so you see… I had no choice… no choice but to…
Ali, Beet & Chalkie:	Bunk!
Corey:	What happened in the end?
Chalkie:	I bunked the afternoon… and the next day took in

45

Section 4

	a ball… a fairly new ball from home… and got someone else to give it to him…
Beet:	You wimp!
Chalkie:	He's got brothers and stuff…
Beet:	You're still a wimp.
Chalkie:	Yeh… but I looked good in those photos for the Agent… sex magnet, Ali said…
Ali:	I didn't!
Chalkie:	Who knows what I'd've looked like if Danzo had got hold of me…
Corey:	Actually… you've reminded me… something similar happened to me… it kind of led me to moving to this school actually.

Section 5: Corey versus the Whole World

Corey:	After I got chucked out of home, I went to live with my Aunt, Mum's sister, Jayne, for a few months. I got on with her really well… she was more like a mum to me than my real Mum. I went to the Drugs councillor… Just once… it was stupid… 'cos I wasn't doing stuff… but he was quite fanciable actually… and then Jane made sure I went to school…
All:	*(Establishing the location with a still image.)* School!
Corey:	*(With sarcasm.)* Yipee!!!
Teacher 1:	Corey Hudson? Well… we are honoured!
Teacher 2:	It's no wonder you don't understand… you're never here.
Teacher 3:	It's not your chair Corey Hudson… let Abigail Goodgirl have it… she sits there now… you sit over here… *(The teachers vocal qualities become increasingly evil – in Corey's mind)* just next to me…
All 3:	*(As though from a horror film.)* On your own…
Corey:	It was a nightmare… I was so behind… in everything… and then…
Deathwish:	*(As a mafia type… if played by Beet a 'girly' wig [pigtails?] should be put worn.)* Not so fast Corey Hudson.
Corey:	Deathwish O'Connor?
Deathwish:	The same.
Corey:	I ain't scared of you.
All:	Everyone was scared of Deathwish O'Connor.
Deathwish:	And why was that…
Little & Big Beanie:	Because you was very, very scary…
Corey:	Deathwish was in the Year below me… and, like Danzo, not particularly big…
Chalkie:	What had you done to upset her then?

Section 5

Corey:	She said I'd…
Deathwish:	… been sarcastic to my mate Beanie… Big Beanie.
Corey:	*(Laughing.)* Big Beanie? I don't even know…
Big Beanie:	You do Corey Hudson…
Corey:	All I said was… was to stop staring…
Deathwish:	No-one tells Big Beanie to stop staring…
Corey:	Well I did!
Deathwish:	You want to say that now… cos she's staring at you!
Big Beanie:	Yeh… tell me now!
Deathwish:	Come on Corey Hudson… tell her to stop staring.
Little Beanie:	I'm staring… and I'm getting really grossed out!
Deathwish:	That's cos what you're staring at is…
Big Beanie:	Gross, Deathwish…
Deathwish:	She's stupid… and if she don't tell you to stop staring…
Corey:	I ain't scared of you…
Deathwish:	Go girls! Get her!
Corey:	*(Creates a still image as though running away. The others exit.)* I ran out of school…
Chalkie:	I bet you were scared?
Corey:	Yeh, scared of what I'd do to her if we did have a fight!
Chalkie:	Go Corey!
Corey:	But I didn't want to let Jayne down… that was important… so I… well I ran to where she worked… I thought she'd be pleased that I hadn't just bunked. When I got there I said…
Chalkie:	Go on:
Corey:	… I remember it as if it was yesterday… *(Now confronting Jayne.)* I'm never going to that bloody school again!

The Gate Escape

Jayne: Corey... what on earth's happened?

Corey: I'm not going back there... it doesn't matter what you say... but I ain't!

Jayne: Corey... I can't just put everything down and...

Corey: What did you want me to do then?

Jayne: I can't talk about it here... not at work love...

Corey: Well I'll go back to the house then... see you later shall I?

Jayne: Corey!

Corey: I could have just gone off round town... I said I wouldn't bunk so I came here... now you can't even be bothered with me.

Jayne: That's not true and you know it isn't... OK... go back home... I'll phone school... and we'll sort it out tonight. *(Corey makes to leave.)* Corey... we can sort it out, can't we?

Corey: I didn't answer.

Jayne: As soon as I got back home she said:

Corey: I'm never going to school again!

Jayne: The next morning I went to try and wake her up and she put her pillow over her face and said:

Corey: I'm never going to school again.

Jayne: In fact if you gave me a pound for every time she said:

Corey: I'm never going to school again!

Jayne: I'd be able to buy out Chelsea Football Club!*

All: I'm never going to school again.

Corey: But I did... Jayne took me in... right in to the School Office and then I'd have to wait for the Head of Year.

---

* Or other topical reference.

49

Section 5

Jayne: I can't be dropping you off everyday Corey…

Corey: I'll be alright after today…

Jayne: Promise you'll stay… just see your Year Head if there are problems.

Corey: Promise.

Jayne: You can do it…

Corey: You've been so…

Jayne: There's no need to say anything… I'm just glad to've helped. You're a lovely girl… just let them see that as well.

Corey: Thanks Jayne.
I even got her a little bottle of perfume… *(Hands it to Jayne.)* to say thank-you… she was really touched by that… I know she was… and all I had to do was stay in school and everything would be alright. Easy eh?

Chalkie: Wrong.

Corey: My Year Head let me stay with her at break times so that I didn't bump into Deathwish…. He was actually really good to me… but it felt all wrong… it was like admitting I was scared… and I wasn't… I could have Deathwish any day…

Chalkie: So what happened then?

Corey: Year Nine SATS… I knew I wasn't going to do very well… so it started all over again.

Chalkie: What?

Corey: The bunking… and the shoplifting… that was something I could do!
It was only a matter of time before Jayne found out… but I thought it'd be longer than it was… on my second day I got back home and Jayne was there. "What are you doing here?"

Jayne: Are you going to tell me where you've been?

Corey: What do you mean?

The Gate Escape

Jayne: Corey, I want you to be straight with me.
Corey: I don't know what you mean.
Jayne: You haven't been to school today.
Corey: And?
Jayne: You promised me.
(Silence.)
Where have you been?
(Silence.)
Let me look in your bag…
Corey: Why?
Jayne: Your books are upstairs… what's in your bag?
Corey: You've been snooping in my room?
Jayne: Have you got something to hide?
Corey: I thought you were different!
Jayne: I thought you were…
Corey: What?
Jayne: I thought you'd keep your promise to me.
Corey: I want to go upstairs.
Jayne: I didn't think you'd break it quite so quickly.
(Corey walks past Jayne on her way upstairs.)
Corey?
Corey: Yeh?
Jayne: What is in your bag?
Corey: What do you think I've been doing?
Jayne: Show me what's in your bag!
(She opens the bag to reveal a shirt, some cd's and some perfume. Jayne picks out the perfume and looks at it.)
I trusted you Corey.
(Silence.)
Corey: Jayne… I'm sorry… really I am.
Jayne: Did you steal the… the one you gave to me?

Section 5

	(Silence.)
Corey:	It spelled the death of our relationship. *(Jayne leaves.)* I was gutted about it… totally! I'd really let her down…
Chalkie:	So what happened next?
Corey:	I went back to Mum's… well it was Dad who really pushed to have me back…
Mike:	She should come back here… I was never happy about her going to Jayne's, it was bound to end in tears… bound to… bloody do-gooder!
Chalkie:	Fairytale reunion?
Corey:	Hardly…
Mike:	This time you'll have me to answer to…
Sue:	*(Under her breath.)* As if that will make any difference.
Mike:	… and if you can't handle it you'll be off to Social Services.
Corey:	Can't we just cut this scene…
Mike:	OK! Shall we skip to the bit where we send you to another school…
Corey:	No… let's do the bit where you two have one of your 'trial separations'!
Mike:	… to another school to try and give her a fresh start.
Corey:	Mum and dad had been arguing a lot…
Sue & Mike:	We were arguing over you!
Corey:	So it's all my fault is it? Nothing to do with your total incompatibility! *(Silence.)* I thought that would shut you up!
Mike:	Then… all of a sudden… Corey came up with… well… with this…
Corey:	OK then… I will change schools… I want a fresh start… but I also want you to promise me

The Gate Escape

	something. I want you to promise that you won't split up with Mum.
Mike :	I… I think it may be too late…
Corey:	Dad… I'm being serious… if you want me to try to start afresh… I want you and Mum to do it too… I want you to at least give it a go…
Sue:	Fair enough… we'll do it… we'll give it a go.
Corey:	So they walked off into the sunset… determined… determined to start a fresh…
Mike /Sue:	A fresh start in our relationship.
Corey:	And a fresh start for me at a new school.
Mike :	Was this… was this just…
Corey & Mike/Sue:	… too much to ask?
Corey:	I had to do loads of catching up to prove to my new school that I was prepared to sort things out… I don't recommend it… it was just copying stuff out… but I did it… for a large part of the Summer holidays…
Mike/Sue:	We were so proud of her…
Sue:	Everything looked as though it was going to be rosy and bright…
Corey:	And… by September… I was ready for the change…

53

Section 6: When Corey Meets Chalkie

Chalkie:	So… Corey came to our school… and there she met… Beet and Alicia… oh, and me of course…. I didn't really hang round with them 'cos by this time my best mate was…
All:	Terry Gale.
Terry:	*(Enters with guitar.)* Superstar guitarist… *(Strikes a chord.)*
All:	All round good guy.
Chalkie:	We'd formed a band in the Summer!
Chalkie & Terry:	Ghostly Grasshoppers.
Corey:	Very seventies.
Chalkie:	My dad thought it was amazing!
Corey:	Exactly!
Chalkie:	We'd practised throughout the summer and had a recording session sorted… I told you I'd be famous!
Chalkie & Terry:	We'll hit the big time! No problem!
Corey:	So how come you were there… on… you know… the day we met?
Chalkie:	It was… I was just leaving assembly… "Terry… I'm going to get really done… I haven't done the homework for Warrener."
Terry:	Nor have I… don't worry about it.
Chalkie:	We'll get a detention though.
Terry:	And?
Chalkie:	My Dad'll go berserk…
Terry:	I can't imagine your dad being like that.
Chalkie:	You don't know my dad… *(Ali walks towards Chalkie.)* What's she want?
Terry:	Who?
Chalkie:	Ali… look…
Ali:	Chalkie… Beet's leaving…
Chalkie:	What?

54

The Gate Escape

Ali: He's leaving… his brother got done over… and well, his mum's already gone… and he's off tomorrow.

Chalkie: What happened?

Ali: He won't talk about it at all.

Chalkie: Where're they off to?

Ali: London.

Chalkie: Blimey!

Ali: We're giving him a send off… lesson after break… at the woods.

Terry: We've got Warrener…

Chalkie: *(To Terry.)* Do you want to come?

Terry: I don't really know him.

Chalkie: I haven't done the homework so…

Terry: Chalkie?

Chalkie: Who else is going?

Ali: Don't know… the usual I suppose.

Chalkie: I dunno…

Terry: Right I'm off…

Chalkie: Wait up Terry…

Terry: I need to go to the loo anyway… see you Chalkie. *(Exits.)*

Ali: Who's the square?

Chalkie: He's alright.

Ali: Come on Chalk… if you haven't done your homework you'll save yourself a detention…

Chalkie: And a rollicking…

Ali: Are you coming then?

Chalkie: I don't know…

Ali: We won't get another chance… with Beet…

Chalkie: That's the problem…

Section 6

Ali:	Why?
Chalkie:	He takes the Mick all the time…
Ali:	That's Beet…
Chalkie:	No… it's…
Ali:	Have it your own way… I thought you'd be up for it… *(She makes to leave.)*
Chalkie:	Ali…
Ali:	What?
Chalkie:	I'll come. It'll be better than facing Warrener. I'll go up to him with the homework tomorrow morning and apologise… he'll be well impressed! *(Exits.)*
Ali:	It was drugs for me… well fags at first… that's what started me off bunking… couldn't have 'em in the classroom so I had to get out. It's strange… by this time… Year 10 some kids had already started to disown us… worried that if they hung round with us they'd get accused of drugs as well… Chalkie was different… there was a history there… but you could see even he was beginning to move away… I hated being on the outside… but I couldn't stop it… We wanted others to come along with us… to make us feel… like better. So when this new girl came… it was… *(Corey enters.)* Target!
Ali:	Do you smoke?
Corey:	Yeh.
Ali:	Do you want to come for a fag?
Corey:	Yeh, alright.
Ali:	As soon as she said yeh… we knew she wasn't exactly a goodie-goodie… so at the end of break I said: "Whatya got?"
Corey:	History.
Ali:	What, with smelly breath Rancid?
Corey:	Actually, that's my dad.
Ali:	What?

The Gate Escape

Corey: *(Pause.)* Only joking…

Ali: You really had me then! What? I bet you'll be in my class… 'cept I'm not going.

Corey: What are you doing then?

Ali: Our mate's leaving tomorrow so we're like saying goodbye to him… it'll be a laugh… there's loads of us going…

Chalkie: 'Loads' translating as Beet, Ali… and me… "Come on Corey… be a blast!" Anyway… I thought it might be good to… you know… get to know you a bit better.

Ali: Don't put her off Chalkie.

Chalkie: You think she'll be able to resist the Chalk boy?

Corey: I'll ignore that…

Ali: No one'll see us.

Chalkie: No, not at the cotch…

Corey: What?

Ali: Our little hideout.

Corey: What?

Chalkie: The teachers won't even know you're in the class…

Ali: You won't be on their registers yet…

Chalkie: So they won't miss you…

Ali: It's up to you Corey…

Chalkie: The bell's going to go in a minute.

Corey: *(On the horn of the dilemma… sighs)* … Oh… bloody hell… my Mum'll go mad if she finds out.

Chalkie: Mine too!

Corey: Come on then!

All: First we had to get out of School.

Section 7: Chalkie's Final Bunk(?) (II)

The Great Escape *MUSIC plays loudly. They undertake a comic 'escape' routine mixing ideas/implements from a typical WWII prison escape to the idea of getting out of school without being seen. In the original production this was done with the assistance of back projections with the cast appearing (initially behind and at the end of the sequence, in front of the screen) in silhouette and various incongruous (in the modern context) props... ropes, wire cutters etc. Eventually they settle, playing as before with the various discarded objects.*

All:	Innocent chatter.
Chalkie:	Big Brother for teenagers.
Beet:	WH Smith's voucher! *(They all laugh raucously and suddenly stop.)*
Corey:	Trapped...
All:	Spot the irony...
Ali:	Cameras...
All:	Spot the fear! Aaaargh!
Chalkie:	Uni-cycle.
All:	Spot the idiot!
Beet:	Vibrant purple vomit! *(He mimes an impressive projectile vomit.)* Wicked!!
Chalkie:	Two quid if you can spot the carrot!
Ali & Beet:	Skin up
Chalkie:	Spot the irresponsible.
Ali & Beet:	Shut it Chalkie!
Ali:	*(Offering Corey a joint.)* Come on Corey...
Beet:	... you know you want to...
All:	Spot the new girl!
Corey:	*(Refusing politely.)* 's alright. *(She takes out a cigarette [mimed] and lights it up.)*
Ali:	*(To Corey.)* You don't say much.

The Gate Escape

Corey:	Not much to say, is there?
Ali:	I thought you'd be a laugh.
Beet:	Chalkie… catch this! *(He hurls an object at Chalkie who catches it.)*
Beet:	*(To Corey.)* How come you changed schools then? No-one comes to this school unless something bad's happened.
Chalkie:	*(Very cheesily!)* Strange name… Corey… *(Clears throat … dramatically)* What's it's history? *(They all look at Chalkie perplexed.)*
Ali & Beet:	What kind of a dumb question is that?
Chalkie:	Oh, but I ask them so masterfully! *(The passage of time sequence is repeated with the 'Ten Minutes later' caption. This time the sequence is noticeably slower.)*
Ali:	The bridge…
Chalkie:	The wooden bridge…
Beet:	The little wooden bridge…
All:	I hate this bridge!
Beet:	Chalkie is a banker!
Corey:	I wish I hadn't come.
Ali & Chalkie:	What did you expect? Ronald MacDonald? *(They all laugh raucously and suddenly stop.)*
Corey:	Babyish… this den…
Ali:	What do you want to do then, Corey?
Beet:	Go back to school if you ain't got the bottle.
Chalkie:	Leave her alone…
Corey:	*(To Chalkie.)* You can shut-up.
Beet:	What's your problem then?
Ali:	You know what I think… I think she's a bloody goody-goody!
Corey:	Goody-goody?

59

Section 7

Ali:	Yeh. I thought 'cos you smoked… you'd be like… a laugh…
Beet:	Goody-goody? What you doing here then?
Chalkie:	Come on Beet… it's her first day.
Ali:	Out of her depth…
Beet:	*(Taunting.)* Not up to hanging with the dudes then Corey?
Corey:	*(To Beet.)* You think you're so big…
Chalkie:	*(Mock Scouse accent.)* Calm down, calm down
Beet:	No. *(To Corey.)* Go on then.
Corey:	Do you really call this fun sitting in a den… you're just little kids…
Beet:	So what does the new girl want to do? We haven't got Barbies to play with… but we could maybe find a Bratz… that's the latest, isn't it?
Corey:	Finished?
Beet:	No I ain't.
Corey:	I'll shut-up then… cos you're so stimulating.
Beet:	Big words for a little girl!
Ali:	What <u>is</u> up with you? Ain't you bunked before?
Beet:	Course she ain't…
Ali:	Well, have you?
Beet:	… you can tell
Corey:	I have…
Beet:	Bull! You're a bloody goody-goody!
Ali:	Don't believe you Corey
Beet:	All mouth and no trousers. Goody-goody!
Chalkie:	I'll walk you back to school if you want… don't listen to them… they're mad.
Beet:	Chalkie's on the pull!

The Gate Escape

Corey:	*(To Chalkie.)* I'll fight my own battles thanks Chalkie!
Beet:	Come on you lot… this is my last day here… I don't want to be spending it with some low-life loser!
Corey:	Who are you calling a loser?
Beet:	Who do you think?
Corey:	Me?
Beet:	Loser!
Corey:	Why?
Beet:	You're scared of bunking!
Corey:	I've bunked loads…
Beet:	Bull!
Corey:	Probably more than you… I even got kicked out of home cos no-one could stop me!
Beet:	Bull! All bull Corey!
Corey:	But I don't just bunk off in a little den… no… I get out and about… have people chasing me… Security Guards… the police… I go nicking… I bet you ain't ever lifted £300 worth of stuff in one day?
Ali:	£300?
Beet:	Don't believe it!
Corey:	It's true!
Beet:	Well, I don't believe it… not unless you can prove it.
Corey:	I don't have to do nothing!
Beet:	Show us what you can do.
Corey:	No…
Beet:	Why not?
Corey:	Not today…
Beet:	Well, I won't be here tomorrow… so come on, let's go into town… now!

Section 7

Chalkie:	I'm not nicking…
Ali:	You won't have to do anything.
Chalkie:	We'll be in town!
Ali:	Come on Chalkie…
Chalkie:	What if we get caught?
Corey:	We won't get caught… trust me!
Beet:	That's more like it… this sounds like a laugh… are you up for it Ali?
Ali:	Yeh… you Chalkie?
Chalkie:	Not sure.
Ali:	So you're going to stay here then, are you…
Ali & Beet:	On your own.
Chalkie:	No, but it'd be just my luck to…
Corey:	Come on Chalkie… it'll be a laugh.
Chalkie:	*(Vocal heartbeats and slow-motion turns to focus on Chalkie, as he decides.)* Alright then… but if we get caught…
Ali, Beet & Corey:	We won't.
Beet:	Wicked!
Chalkie:	And before I knew where I was… we were all off… out of the cotch and… on our way into town.
Ali, Beet & Corey:	Chalkie… come on! Won't you ever stop narrating? *(They exit.)*
Chalkie:	So there we were… in the town centre… when suddenly…
Voice:	*(Amplified with echo and high volume.)* Hello Chalkie… Hello Corey. I am here to deliver the Big Bother to end your morning's truancy…
Chalkie:	Haven't we been here before?
Voice:	Fate has decided to whom the ending should occur.
Chalkie:	Come on, who is it?

The Gate Escape

	(Silence.)
Voice:	Are you ready? *(Silence.)*
All:	Yes.
Voice:	Are you quite sure?
Voice:	We're certain…
Chalkie:	Come on…
Others:	Shut-up Chalkie!
Voice:	Remember… Fate has decided who should face the Big Bother. There shall be no arguments.
All:	Get on with it!
Voice:	The one selected for Big Bother this morning is…
All:	Come on!
Corey:	It's gonna be me I know it is!
Chalkie:	No, it'll be me.
Others:	Shut up Chalkie! *(Silence.)*
Chalkie:	Come on!
Voice:	*(Pause.)* Chalkie.
Chalkie:	Oh my… !!!
Others:	What?
Chalkie:	Why? *(The following sequence could be pre-filmed and shown on the screen.)*
Chalkie:	I don't consider myself to be someone who 'proper' bunks really…
Other 3:	Come on Chalkie… won't you ever stop narrating. *(Chalkie turns to run with them.)*
Chalkie:	I'd only choose to bunk… if I needed to avoid some embarrassment… or trouble…
Other 3:	Last one in the water's a plonker! *(They run off.)*

Section 7

	The amplified sound of someone passing wind.)
Mrs Picklewitch:	Distracting Peter Performer?
Chalkie:	Wasn't me Miss.
Mrs Picklewitch:	At least own up and be honest.
Chalkie:	The next day I bunked her lesson and then stayed off for the whole day in case she saw me… *(Laughs.)* …but I got away with it.
Mrs Picklewitch:	*(With clenched fists.)* …And got away with it!!!
All:	*(A Message Alert bleeps loudly. This could alternatively be flashed up letter by letter on the screen.)* **Danzo wants 2 fight u 2moro**
Chalkie:	Aaaargh!
Ali:	You got to face him Chalkie!
Chalkie:	No way… I'm not having some little Year Seven beat me up… See ya.
Ali:	*(If presented live, Ali grabs Chalkie preventing him from leaving)*… Beets send off… are you coming?
Chalkie:	It'll be better than facing Warrener without my homework.
All:	Go Chalkie!
Voice:	Chalkie… this has led you to face… the Big Bother.
Chalkie:	Can't I appeal?
Voice:	No.
Chalkie:	But you could have found just as many reasons to choose Corey.
Voice:	That is totally correct.
Chalkie:	So why me? Cos I'm a boy?
Voice:	Corey has landed herself in big bother before, and will no doubt again… Fate is keen to see you having to deal with this situation…
Chalkie:	But that wasn't the task.

The Gate Escape

Voice:	Fate reserves the right to change the rules… our agenda is different to yours… the decision is final… but just before you leave Chalkie to face his Big Bother… we have a "reward" for you.
All:	Wow!
Chalkie:	That's not fair!
Beet:	A Chinese take-away… it's always a Chinese take-away… wow… bunk off school and get a Chinese take-away…
Voice:	No. The reward will be played on the video screen.
Corey:	Not our parents?
Ali:	That wouldn't be a reward!
Voice:	The reward will be a glimpse into your future.
All:	What?
Voice:	A look at what is to come of you all.
Beet:	I don't want to see.
Corey & Ali:	Go on Beet.
Beet:	No… don't want to.
Voice:	If you don't want to see… you may leave.
Chalkie:	Can I leave too?
All & Voice:	No way… Chalkay *(sic)*!
Beet:	What… so I go right now.
Voice:	If that is what you want.
Beet:	Yeh… I do… I don't want to know what's going to happen to me! See you guys. Trust me… you shouldn't accept this reward… you'll regret it! *(Goes to exit.)*
Ali:	Will *we* get to hear what happened to Beet?
Voice:	If you wish.
Beet:	*(Turns back.)* That can't be right.

Section 7

Chalkie:	Now who's getting all worried?
Beet:	Shut it Chalkie!
Corey:	This is creepy.
Voice:	Beet… are you staying… or going?
Beet:	I'm off… *(He exits.)* Bye you lot…
All:	Bye Beet… look after yourself.
Beet:	Wicked!
Voice:	Run VCR *(Ali appears on the screen costumed as a stereotypical [comical] elderly person.)*
Corey:	Look Ali… that's you.
Ali:	It ain't!
Corey:	It is.
Ali & Chalkie:	Sshhh
Elderly Ali:	*(On screen.)* I bet this is a bit of a shock
Ali:	Is that me?
All & Voice:	Yes.
Ali:	This is well weird… look at those wrinkles!
Ali & Chalkie:	Sshhh
Elderly Ali:	*(On screen.)* Schooldays… Oh, I remember them well! I didn't stop bunking till my Mum got these letters at the end of Year 10… threatening to take her to court. She was worried they'd send her to prison… No one much talks to you when you haven't been in school for a while and I felt so thick… just sat there in the lessons. But gradually, I started to get on with people better… like at Junior school… when I was really popular. Me and Beet were like known as the hardest in the year… we used to like that reputation… but… well… after he moved… something happened to him… and it… stopped me doing drugs… well not stopped exactly… but… made me cut down. I ended up with about 75% attendance in year 11. I got E's

The Gate Escape

	and F's. It was OK. I became a hairdresser. Regrets… we all have 'em I suppose… but yeh… sometimes it annoys me what I did to my life. *(The image freezes.)*
Ali:	That is so freaky! And that bit about Beet… what was that all about?
Corey:	Yeh… I don't know if I want to see mine… not after that…
Ali:	Come on… I did.
Chalkie:	I wish I could see mine. *(The screen shows the 10-0 countdown indicating a new VCR is about to begin.)*
Ali & Corey:	Sshhh
Corey:	Oh no! *(Hides her face but Ali pulls her hands down making her look.)*
Elderly Corey:	*(Corey is dressed up to be an elderly person… with a comic hairdo!)* Hello!
Corey:	Go away… I don't want to see.
Chalkie:	*(On screen.)* Like the hair Corey!
Ali & Corey:	Shut it Chalkie!
Elderly Corey:	*(On screen.)* I bet you didn't expect to see me looking like this! Like the hair?
Corey:	No I don't!
Ali & Corey:	Sshhh
Elderly Corey:	*(On screen.)* I bet you're going to be surprised by this… but it's all true…
Corey:	Please don't let it be scary!
Elderly Corey:	*(On screen.)* About January in my year 10, I started watching programmes on TV about how they calmed down naughty kids. It gave me the idea of being a psychiatrist… and… well… I just stopped bunking 'cos I needed the grades. Actually, I changed the game… I was still accused of doing stuff so it became fun to be able to prove to the

67

Section 7

	teachers that I hadn't been involved… it gave me a sort of motivation to prove them wrong! *(Laughing.)* …but it was hard. I'd stay in three, four nights a week working to catch up… but I did it… I got my grades and I became a psychiatrist… I guess I was unusual… I guess I was lucky! *(The screen freezes.)*
Ali:	That wasn't so bad.
Corey:	It's weird… do you think it's true?
Ali:	It can't be…
Corey:	I don't know… it maybe like a vision of what could happen… it can't all be sorted out…
Ali:	But Beet?
Corey:	Ask the voice then… go on… it said we could find out…
Ali:	*(Calling out.)* Disembodied Voice!
Voice:	Yes.
Ali:	Can we ask a question?
Voice:	You just did.
Ali:	No, I'm being serious… what happened to Beet?
Voice:	On the 25th January 200…? *(Update the year annually… the date is fictional)* …Beet never settled into his new school. He…
Ali:	*(Looking back.)* …he mucked up didn't he?
Voice:	He really messed up. You've got to understand… your stories are based on real ones… so we can't fake the ending… no one ever saw Beet again. And no-one from your area ever really found out what happened. I'm sorry but that's how it is.
Ali:	*(Shocked.)* Wow! I'm glad Beet didn't stay around to hear that… he'd've freaked!
Chalkie:	What about me… Can't I hear what's going to happen to me?
Voice:	Your future is still in the hands of Fate… we have

The Gate Escape

	to see how you react to your first spot of Big Bother.
Chalkie:	I won't ever bunk again… that's for sure.
Voice:	I don't know if I believe you!
Chalkie:	I won't. Honest I won't… I'll do anything!
Voice:	Even a stupid dance.
Chalkie:	Yes anything!
Voice:	Too late for that Chalkie…
Chalkie:	What?
Voice:	Far too late for that Chalkie… Ali and Corey… in a moment you must leave… leave Chalkie alone to face…
Ali:	Dah dah der!!!
Voice:	*(With Echo.)* …The Big Bother!
Chalkie:	Noooooooo!
Voice:	Let the Big Bother begin!
Chalkie:	Oh no!!! Look!
Others:	Where?
Chalkie:	There! *(Chalkie is frozen to the spot.)*
Beet:	*(Laughing.)* It's wicked… when you're chased by the police… you just feel so giggly and…
Ali:	… and when you get away you just think…
Ali, Beet & Corey:	That was BAD! That was rude!
Beet:	You think you're never going to get caught…
Ali:	You do get away…
Ali, Beet & Corey:	… most times. *(They run to different areas… Chalkie remains frozen.)*
Chalkie:	*(Petrified.)* Old Bill!!!
Corey:	Truancy sweep…
Ali, Beet & Corey:	Leg it!!!

Section 7

Chalkie:	There's me… just kind of rooted to the spot.
Ali, Beet & Corey:	Chalkie!
Chalkie:	Unable to move.
Others:	Chalkie!!!
Chalkie:	Thinking… this isn't fair!
Others:	What are you doing Chalk?
Chalkie:	This shouldn't be happening to me… well, should it? Look at them… they're always bunking… why can't they be rooted to the spot like some stupid rooted to the spot thing?
Ali:	Leave him…
Beet:	This is such a laugh! Chalkie in the shit!
Chalkie:	I'm not tempted to giggle!
Corey:	If I told you I'd got some of my Granny's fruitcake… would you come?
Chalkie:	No, actually I want to stay here to be arrested… I get quite a thrill from those leather gloves pressing down on my shoulders and the feel of a truncheon around my head! What do you think?
All 3:	We're off!
Chalkie:	Wait… please!!! Ali!!! Wait!
All 3:	To infinity and beyond!!! *(They exit.)*
Chalkie:	*(Music strikes up.)* …Why me? This is so unfair. *(There is a stylised comic chase sequence. Finally two police Officers ensnare the still immobile Chalkie.)* It's fine… I'll come without a struggle… no need for handcuffs… take me… I'm yours…
Police:	Nicked!
Chalkie:	Right now they've got me, what am I going to say? *(Starting off in a 'BBC' voice that gradually becomes more desperate and with increasing speed.)* "Right Officer… I only took a little time out to say

The Gate Escape

farewell to a companion at school. They were smoking joints but I wasn't… it was them… it was all them you should be talking to, not me… I don't normally bunk off… surely you'll take these factors into consideration and let me go back to school and can't you just forget that it's happened?"
No… no… it doesn't sound good enough for the police… not serious enough.
"I hadn't done my History homework and I was truly frightened of Mr Warrener for getting cross with me."
Still doesn't sound too good. does it… maybe I'll just apologise…
"I'm sorry… I'm really sorry… I won't do it again… I promise… only don't tell my mum and dad else my dad'll ban me from playing with my band… see… I've always wanted to be on telly and…

Police:	Always wanted to be on telly eh?
Chalkie:	Yeh… always… I've got an agent… and I'm in this band… Ghostly Grasshoppers….
Police:	*(Approving.)* Very Seventies.
Chalkie:	It's like a step on the ladder.
Police:	So, are we to presume that you've always wanted to be famous?
Chalkie:	This is a strange line of questioning… what's going on?
Police:	Always wanted to be on the telly?
Chalkie:	Yes. Why are you asking?
Police:	We've got a nice surprise for you.
Chalkie:	From round the corner…
Police:	Previously hidden from view….
Chalkie:	And completely unsighted by me
TV 1:	Was a TV crew from…
All:	The local BBC News!!!!
Chalkie:	*(Squirming with embarrassment.)* Oooooooh.

Section 7

TV 1:	Cameras rolling….
TV 2:	Take one…
TV 1:	Nice angle…
TV 2:	Boy looks so embarrassed…
Police:	Nice smile for the camera sonny!
Chalkie:	*(Still being helped up by the Police for the Cameras and audience to 'see'.)* I just kept thinking "Oh no!" my face is going to be shown round the whole of the UK. Why me? I don't deserve this. *(The Police Officer deposits Chalkie in what he makes out to be a very small space.)* They bought me back to school in a meat wagon… they had tiny, tiny little cages and they're really small… locked up like a dog with no room to manoeuvre…
Beet:	By the time they brought him back… we were outside…
Ali, Corey & Beet:	Laughing… silently so no one would hear us!
Chalkie:	It was so embarrassing.
Ali:	And he got done…
Beet:	Really done…
Chalkie:	At home that night… my Mum was watching the news…
Ali, Corey & Beet:	They blurred his face out.
Chalkie:	But everyone recognised me… even my Nan recognised me.
Beet:	*(Pretending to be Chalkie's Nan adopting suitable stereotypical voice… using a hanky over his head as a headscarf.)* It was so obviously you… the way you walked… it was obvious!
Chalkie:	She didn't stop going on!
Beet (as Nan):	You're not going to get the grades you want… They'll be proper messed up and you'll not get a

The Gate Escape

	good job with lots of money.
Chalkie:	Every time she saw me…
Beet (as Nan):	Now it's bunking… next you'll be suspended… then it'll be prison…
Chalkie:	Every time she saw anyone.
Beet (as Nan):	My little Shirley…
Ali:	Shirley?
Corey:	That's a girl's name…
Chalkie:	It's after a Wrestler if you must know… hardly anyone calls me it.
Beet (as Nan):	My little Shirley… he was on the TV the other day…
Corey:	*(Adopting the role of one of Nan's old friends.)* Oh was he… what was that in then? Blue Peter?
Beet (as Nan):	No.
Corey (as Nan's Friend):	Telly-Tubbies?
Beet (as Nan):	No.
Corey (as Nan's Friend):	*(Becoming very excited.)* Top of the Pops?
Beet (as Nan):	No!
Corey (as Nan's Friend):	Newsround?
Beet (as Nan):	Actually… by some amazing quirk of fate you're getting warmer.
Corey (as Nan's Friend):	Oh? Quirk of fate eh?
Beet (as Nan):	It was The Local News… Truancy sweep.
Corey (as Nan's Friend):	Oooh my gawd… He always said he'd been on telly, didn't he?
Chalkie:	Shut up going on about it Nan! Up until that time I'd always wanted to be

73

Section 7

	famous… I tell you… it's not all it's cracked up to be… 'cos that was it for me… my fifteen minutes of fame…
Voice:	But Chalkie… did you ever bunk again?
Chalkie:	I'm not saying… but… *(To audience.)* well, what do you think? **Music.**

If you have enjoyed reading and/or working with this playscript, you may like to find out about other plays we publish. There are brief descriptions and other details on the following pages.

All plays deal with contemporary social and moral issues and are suitable for Youth Theatres, Schools, Colleges, and adult AmDram. They are ideal for GCSE Drama/English exam use and frequently do well in One Act Play Festivals. They offer both male and female performers equally challenging opportunities.

For enquiries or to order plays published by *dbda*, please contact Bharti Bhikha or Manna Tailor,
dbda, Pin Point, Rosslyn Crescent, Harrow HA1 2SB.
Tel: 0870 333 7771
Fax: 0870 333 7772
Email: info@dbda.co.uk

All enquiries regarding performing rights of plays by *Mark Wheeller*, should be made to:
Meg Davis, MBA Literary Agents,
62 Grafton Way, London W1P 5LD.
Tel: 020 7387 2076
E-mail: meg@mbalit.co.uk

All enquiries regarding performing rights of 'Heroin Lies' by *Wayne Denfhy*, should be made to:
Wayne Denfhy, c/o *dbda*,
Pin Point, Rosslyn Crescent, Harrow HA1 2SB.
Tel: 0870 333 7771
Email: info@dbda.co.uk (subject: Wayne Denfhy)

Other plays published by *dbda*

Legal Weapon by Mark Wheeller
ISBN 1 902843 01 0
Cast: 2m & 2f with doubling, or 1f, 3m & 13
Duration: 60 minutes   KS 4 to adult

A fictional story using oral testimony of RTA offenders and victim families, Legal Weapon tells the story of a young man's relationship with his girlfriend – and his car. Both are flawed, but his speeding causes the loss of a life and the loss of his freedom. Fast, funny and very powerful.

'To write in the language of late teenagers is a fine example of high artistic accomplishment.'

David Lippiett, Guild of Drama Adjudicators

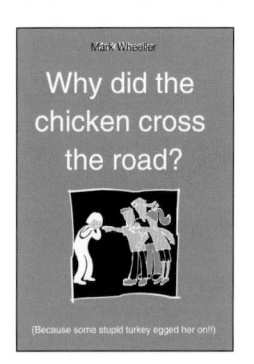

Price: £ 5.50 per book
£70.00 for a set of 15

Why did the chicken cross the road? by Mark Wheeller
ISBN 1 902843 00 2
Cast: 2m & 2f with doubling, or 3f, 3m & 3
Duration: 35 minutes   KS 3 & 4

The story of two cousins, Tammy and Chris. Tammy gets killed in a stupid game of 'chicken' on the one morning that the cousins do not cycle to school. Chris, unable to tell anyone else about his part in the accident, has to live with this dreadful secret.

'An imaginative and moving look at risk taking at a time when peer pressure is at its strongest.'

Rosie Welch, LARSOA

Price: £ 5.50 per book
£70.00 for a set of 15

Too Much Punch for Judy by Mark Wheeller
ISBN 1 902843 05 3
Cast: 2m & 2f with doubling, or 3f, 3m & 6
Duration: 50 minutes   KS 4 to adult

A hard-hitting documentary play, based on a tragic drink-drive accident that results in the death of Jo, front seat passenger. The driver, her sister Judy, escapes unhurt (or has she?). This play has become one of the most frequently performed plays ever!

'The play will have an impact on young people or adults. It will provoke discussion. It stimulates and wants you to cry out for immediate social action and resolution.'

Henry Shankula - Addiction Research Foundation, Toronto

Price: £ 5.50 per book
£70.00 for a set of 15

Hard to Swallow by Mark Wheeller
ISBN 1 902843 08 8

Cast: *3f & 2m with doubling, or 6f, 3m & 16*
Duration: *70 minutes*   KS 3 to adult

This play is an adaptation of Maureen Dunbar's award winning book (and film) **Catherine** which charts her daughter's uneven battle with anorexia and the family's difficulties in coping with the illness.

'This play reaches moments of almost unbearable intensity... naturalistic scenes flow seamlessly into sequences of highly stylised theatre... such potent theatre!'

Vera Lustiq – The Independent

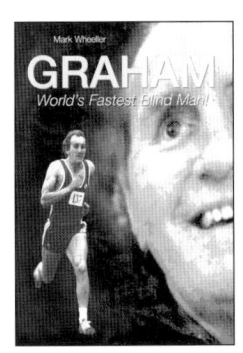

Price: £ 5.50 per book
£70.00 for a set of 15

GRAHAM – World's Fastest Blind Man! by Mark Wheeller
ISBN 1 902843 09 6

Cast: *5m & 4f with doubling, or up to 34*
Duration: *80 minutes*   KS 3/4 to adult

A play full of lively humour telling the inspirational story of Graham Salmon MBE. Totally blind since birth, Graham went on to become the World's Fastest Blind Man running 100 metres in 11.4 seconds! The play, written in Mark's unique documentary style, skillfully brings to life Graham's courage, tenacity and wonderful sense of humour.

'Very good, very moving, very very funny!'

Bruce Henderson, Principal Teacher of Drama,
Wester Hailes Education Centre, Edinburgh

Price: £ 5.50 per book
£70.00 for a set of 15

Dan Nolan – Missing (based on a true story) by Mark Wheeller
ISBN 1 902843 10 X

Cast: *2m & 2f with doubling, or up to 18*
Duration: *55 minutes*   KS 3/4 to adult

A play based on the tragic case of Dan Nolan, a teenage boy who went missing on the night of January 1st 2002. His family continue their search to discover what happened that night. The play, in the same documentary style as 'Too Much Punch for Judy', is written in the belief that something good can emerge from something so tragic.

'Unusual and deeply affecting. Skillfully written... achieves astonishing depth and authenticity... addresses a wound still raw and stands up as a fitting testament to a young life.'

Charles Evans, Adjudicator – Eastleigh Drama Festiv~'

Price: £ 5.50 per book
£70.00 for a set of 15

Wacky Soap – *a Musical with a difference...*

The story of Wacky Soap, by Mark Wheeller, first appeared as a full **Musical play**. The play script of the full version includes scheme of work for KS3/4 and is shown on the opposite page. A mini version of the play is included with the **Music Score**.

The Story of Wacky Soap (shown opposite) by Mark & Rachel Wheeller, is a beautifully illustrated book with the story in prose form. It's often used as inspiration with props and costumes when producing the play.

A **Past-performance CD** gives you the opportunity to hear the songs of the play, while a fully orchestrated **Backing track CD** will be invaluable to those who want to produce the play but do not have music facilities.

**Wacky Soap –
The Music Score and
Mini Musical**
ISBN 1 902843 06 1

A companion book, includes a Mini-Musical version of the play.

Mini-Musical Duration:
40 mins

Price: £ 4.95 per book
£65.00 for a set of 15

Past performance CD
Price: £15.00 each

Backing track CD
Price: £25.00 each

"Wacky Soap' was an outstanding success!!!... We have had letters from people in the audience saying what a fab show it was and how impressed they were. The most frequent comment was that it was a 'risk' to put it on as a school show (as opposed to doing 'Oliver' or 'Little Shop of Horrors') and one that thoroughly paid off!!
'The feel good factor was amazing' was another comment we had. Many people said how impressed they were by the 'community' spirit of the production – everybody working together without the 'star' element creeping in!"

John Plant, Head of Drama, Southmoor School, Sunderland

...ays by Mark Wheeller

... of Love

Script: Graham Cole & Mark Wheeller
Duration: 100 mins
Cast: 25 (11f, 8m & 6m/f)

A bi-lingual play (80% English & 20% French) about teenage pregnancy. Lucy is fourteen - she hopes to become a vet and is working hard to gain good grades in her GCSE exams, when she discovers she is pregnant. She faces a series of major decisions, not least of which is what to tell the father... Ideal as a school production and Key Stage 4 Drama course book.

Sweet FA !

Script: Mark Wheeller
Duration: 45 mins plus interval
Cast: 3f / 2m (or more)
Published by: SchoolPlay Productions Ltd. Tel: 01206 540111

A Zigger Zagger for girls (and boys)! A new play (also available as a full length Musical) telling the true life story of Southampton girl footballer Sarah Stanbury (Sedge) whose ambition is to play Football (Soccer) for England. Her dad is delighted ... her mum disapproves strongly! An ideal GCSE production and Key Stage 4 Drama course book. Drama GCSE scheme of work also available.

Blackout – One Evacuee in Thousands   MUSICAL

Script: Mark Wheeller with the Stantonbury Youth Theatre   **Music:** Mark Wheeller
Duration: 90 mins plus interval   **Published by:** SchoolPlay Productions Ltd.

A Musical about the plight of Rachel Eagle, a fictional evacuee in World War II. Rachel's parents are determined that the war will not split the family up. After refusing to have her evacuated in 1939 they decide to do so midway though 1940. At first Rachel does not settle but, after the death of her mother, she becomes increasingly at home with her billets in Northamptonshire. When her father requests that she return she wants to stay where she feels at home. An ideal large scale school production with good parts for girls (and boys).

The Most Absurd Xmas (Promenade?) Musical in the World...Ever!

Script: Lyndsey Adams, Michael Johnston, Stuart White & Mark Wheeller   **Cast:** Big!
Music: James Holmes   **Duration:** 100 mins
Published by: SchoolPlay Productions Ltd. Tel: 01206 540111

Eat your heart out Ionesco! If you want a musical with a message ... don't consider this one! Santa fails to arrive one year in the Bower of Bliss. Why not? A shortage of carrots perhaps? Or is it because the central character is forbidden to use her musical gift, and whose parents disguise her as a cactus? It all ends reasonably happily and is a bundle of laughs. Originally conceived as a Promenade production. An ideal large scale school Christmas production or alternative an "absurd" summer production.

For more details and an up-to-date list of plays, please visit Mark's website:
www.amdram.co.uk/wheellerplays *(please note wheeller has two "l")*

All enquiries regarding performing rights should be made to: Meg Davis, MBA Literary Agents, 62 Grafton Way, London W1P 5LD. Tel: 020 7387 2076. E-mail: meg@mbalit.co.uk